Exploring the Unknown: Selected Documents in the History of the U.S. Civil Space Program, Organizing for Exploration, Volume I

National Aeronautics and Space Administration (NASA)

The BiblioGov Project is an effort to expand awareness of the public documents and records of the U.S. Government via print publications. In broadening the public understanding of government and its work, an enlightened democracy can grow and prosper. Ranging from historic Congressional Bills to the most recent Budget of the United States Government, the BiblioGov Project spans a wealth of government information. These works are now made available through an environmentally friendly, print-on-demand basis, using only what is necessary to meet the required demands of an interested public. We invite you to learn of the records of the U.S. Government, heightening the knowledge and debate that can lead from such publications.

Included are the following Collections:

Budget of The United States Government
Presidential Documents
United States Code
Education Reports from ERIC
GAO Reports
History of Bills
House Rules and Manual
Public and Private Laws

Code of Federal Regulations
Congressional Documents
Economic Indicators
Federal Register
Government Manuals
House Journal
Privacy act Issuances
Statutes at Large

NASA SP-4407

EXPLORING THE UNKNOWN

Selected Documents in the History of the
U.S. Civil Space Program
Volume I: Organizing for Exploration

John M. Logsdon, Editor
with Linda J. Lear, Jannelle Warren-Findley,
Ray A. Williamson, and Dwayne A. Day

The NASA History Series

National Aeronautics and Space Administration
NASA History Office
Washington, D.C.   1995

Library of Congress Cataloguing-in-Publication Data

Exploring the Unknown: Selected Documents in the History of the U.S. Civil Space
Program / John M. Logsdon, editor with Linda J. Lear... [et al.]
p. cm.—(The NASA history series) (NASA SP: 4407)

     Includes bibliographical references and indexes.
     Contents: v. 1. Organizing for exploration
     1. Astronautics—United States--History.   I. Logsdon, John M., 1937-   .
II. Lear, Linda J., 1940- .   III. Series.   IV. Series: NASA SP: 4407.
TL789.8.U5E87   1995   95-9066
387.8'0973—dc20   CIP

Chapter Four

Documents

Contents

Chapter Two

Essay: "Origins of U.S. Space Policy: Eisenhower, Open Skies, and Freedom of Space," by R. Cargill Hall

Documents

Chapter Three

Documents

Acknowledgments

The idea for creating a reference work that would include documents seminal to the evolution of the civilian space program of the United States came from then-NASA Chief Historian Sylvia K. Kraemer. She recognized that while there were substantial primary resources for future historians and others interested in the early years of the U.S. space programs available in many archives, and particularly in the NASA Historical Reference Collection of the History Office at NASA Headquarters in Washington, D.C., this material was widely scattered and contained a mixture of the significant and the routine. It was her sense that it was important to bring together the "best" of this documentary material in a widely accessible form. This collection, and any long-term value it may have, is first of all the result of that vision. Once Dr. Kraemer left her position as NASA Chief Historian to assume broader responsibilities within the agency, the project was guided with a gentle but firm hand by her successor, Roger D. Launius. Without his subtle prodding and supportive advice, the undertaking might have taken even longer than it has to reach closure.

Jannelle Warren-Findley, an independent intellectual/cultural historian, and Linda J. Lear, an adjunct professor of history at George Washington University, approached the Space Policy Institute of George Washington University's Elliott School of International Affairs with the suggestion that it might serve as the institutional base for a proposal to NASA to undertake the documentary history project. This suggestion found a positive response; the Space Policy Institute was created in 1987 as a center of scholarly research and graduate education regarding space issues, and as a resource for those interested in a knowledgeable but independent perspective on past and current space activities. Having the kind of historical base that would have to be created to carry out the documentary history project would certainly enhance the Institute's capabilities, and so the Space Policy Institute joined with Warren-Findley, Lear, and Ray A. Williamson of the congressional Office of Technology Assessment in preparing a proposal to NASA. Much to our delight, we were awarded the contract for the project in late 1988, and the enterprise got officially under way in May 1989.

The undertaking proved more challenging than anyone had anticipated. The combination of getting ourselves started in the right direction, canvassing and selecting from the immense documentary resources available, commissioning essays to introduce the various sections of the work from external authors and writing several essays ourselves, and dealing with conflicting demands on the time of the four principals in the project has led to a delay in publishing the volume beyond what we anticipated when first undertaking the project. The final pieces of the manuscript for this volume were not delivered to NASA until the end of 1993. By that time, both Jannelle Warren-Findley and Linda Lear had moved on to the next steps in their careers, and Ray Williamson, who had taken a nine-month leave from the Office of Technology Assessment in 1990 to work on the project, had long ago returned to his primary job. This meant that Warren-Findley and Lear did not have the opportunity to make the kinds of contribution to the final product for which they had hoped; nevertheless, without their initiative, the effort would not have been located at George Washington University, and they both made crucial contributions to conceptualizing and organizing the work in its early stages. For that, they deserve high credit. Ray Williamson has been able to stay involved with the project on an occasional basis since returning to the Office of Technology Assessment, and he has made important contributions to several sections of the effort.

In its start-up phase, the project profited from the advice of a distinguished advisory panel that met twice formally; members of the panel were also always available for individual consultation. Included on this panel were: Carroll W. Pursell, Jr., Case Western University (chair); Charlene Bickford, First Congress Project; Herbert Friedman, Naval Research Laboratory; Richard P. Hallion, Air Force Historian; John Hodge, NASA (retired); Sally Gregory Kohlstedt, University of Minnesota; W. Henry Lambright, Syracuse University;

Sharon Thibodeau, National Archives and Records Administration; and John Townsend, NASA (retired). Certainly, none of these individuals bear responsibility for the final content or style of this work, but their advice along the way was invaluable.

We owe thanks to the individuals and organizations that have searched their files for potentially useful materials, and for the staffs at various archives and collections who have helped us locate documents. Without question, first among them is Lee D. Saegesser of the History Office at NASA Headquarters, who has helped compile the NASA Historical Reference Collection that contains many of the documents selected for inclusion in this work. All those who in the future will write on the history of the U.S. space program will owe a debt of thanks to Lee; those who have already worked in this area realize his tireless contributions.

Essential to the project was a system for archiving the documents collected. Charlene Bickford, on the basis of her experience with the First Congress Project, advised on our approach to archiving and to developing document headnotes. The archiving system was developed by graduate student John Morris, who also assisted with document collection. The documentary archive has been nurtured with fervor by another graduate student, Dwayne A. Day; Dwayne has made many major contributions to all aspects of the project. Other students who have worked on the project since its inception include Max Nelson, Jordan Katz, Stewart Money, Michelle Heskett, Robin Auger, and Heather Young. All have been a great help.

Beginning with Linda Lear, a series of individuals has struggled to bring editorial consistency to the essays and headnotes introducing the documents included in this work, and to develop an initial version of the work's index. They have included Erica Angst, Kathie Pett Keel, and, during the final two years of completing this volume, particularly Kimberly Carter. Their contributions have been essential to the lasting quality of the end product. Alita Black also helped set up the indexing system.

There are numerous people at NASA associated with historical study, technical information, and the mechanics of publishing who helped in myriad ways in the preparation of this documentary history. J.D. Hunley, of the NASA History Office, edited and critiqued the text before he departed to take over the History Program at the Dryden Flight Research Center; and his replacement, Stephen J. Garber, prepared the index and helped in the final proofing of the work. Nadine Andreassen of the NASA History Office performed editorial and proofreading work on the project; and the staffs of the NASA Headquarters Library, the Scientific and Technical Information Program, and the NASA Document Services Center provided assistance in locating and preparing for publication the documentary materials in this work. The NASA Headquarters Printing and Design Office developed the layout and handled printing. Specifically, we wish to acknowledge the work of Jane E. Penn, Angela M. La Croix, Patricia M. Talbert, and Jonathan L. Friedman for their editorial and design work. In addition, Michael Crnkovic, Craig A. Larsen, and Larry J. Washington saw the book through the publication process.

Finally, the staff of the Space Policy Institute—Kim Lutz, Paul McDonnell, and Flo Williams—have facilitated the effort throughout.

Introduction

One of the most important developments of the twentieth century has been the movement of humanity into space with machines and people. The underpinnings of that movement—why it took the shape it did; which individuals and organizations were involved; what factors drove a particular choice of scientific objectives and technologies to be used; and the political, economic, managerial, and international contexts in which the events of the space age unfolded—are all important ingredients of this epoch transition from an Earthbound to a spacefaring people. This desire to understand the development of spaceflight in the United States sparked this documentary history.

The extension of human activity into outer space has been accompanied by a high degree of self-awareness of its historical significance. Few large-scale activities have been as extensively chronicled so closely to the time they actually occurred. Many of those who were directly involved were quite conscious that they were making history, and they kept full records of their activities. Because most of the activity in outer space was carried out under government sponsorship, it was accompanied by the documentary record required of public institutions, and there has been a spate of official and privately written histories of most major aspects of space achievement to date. When top leaders considered what course of action to pursue in space, their deliberations and decisions often were carefully put on the record. There is, accordingly, no lack of material for those who aspire to understand the origins and early evolution of U.S. space policies and programs.

This reality forms the rationale for this compilation. Precisely because there is so much historical material available on space matters, the National Aeronautics and Space Administration (NASA) decided in 1988 that it would be extremely useful to have easily available to scholars and the interested public a selective collection of many of the seminal documents related to the evolution of the U.S. civilian space program up to that time. While recognizing that much space activity has taken place under the sponsorship of the Department of Defense and other national security organizations, the U.S. private sector, and in other countries around the world, NASA felt that there would be lasting value in a collection of documentary material primarily focused on the evolution of the U.S. government's civilian space program, most of which has been carried out since 1958 under the agency's auspices. As a result, the NASA History Office contracted with the Space Policy Institute of George Washington University's Elliott School of International Affairs to prepare such a collection, with a 1988 cutoff date for documents to be included. This volume and two additional ones detailing programmatic developments and relations with other organizations that will follow are the result.

The documents collected in this research project were assembled from a diverse number of both public and private sources. A major repository of primary source materials relative to the history of the civil space program is the NASA Historical Reference Collection of the NASA History Office located at the agency's Washington headquarters. Project assistants combed this collection for the "cream" of the wealth of material housed there. Indeed, one purpose of this work from the start was to capture some of the highlights of the holdings at headquarters. Historical materials housed at the other NASA installations, and at institutions of higher learning such as Rice University, Rensselaer Polytechnic Institute, and Virginia Polytechnic University, were also mined for their most significant materials. Other collections from which documents have been drawn include the Eisenhower, Kennedy, Johnson, and Carter Presidential Libraries; the papers of T. Keith Glennan, Thomas O. Paine, James C. Fletcher, George M. Low, and John A. Simpson; and the archives of the National Academy of Sciences, the Rand Corporation, AT&T, the Communications Satellite Corporation, INTELSAT, the Jet Propulsion Laboratory of the California Institute of Technology, and the National Archives and Records Administration.

Copies of more than 2,000 documents in their original form collected during this project (not just the documents selected for inclusion), as well as a data base that provides a guide to their contents, have been deposited in the NASA Historical Reference Collection. Another complete set of project materials is located at the Space Policy Institute at George Washington University. These materials in their original forms are available for use by researchers seeking additional information about the evolution of the U.S. civil space program.

The documents selected for inclusion in this volume are presented in four major sections, each covering a particular aspect of the evolution of U.S. space policies and programs. Those sections address: the antecedents to the U.S. space program; the origins of U.S. space policy in the Eisenhower era; the evolution of U.S. space policies and plans; and the organization of the civilian space effort. A second volume of this work will contain documents arranged in four sections addressing specific relations with other organizations: the NASA/industry/university nexus; civil-military space cooperation; international space cooperation; and NASA, commercialization in space, and communications satellites. A third volume will describe programmatic developments: human spaceflight; space science; Earth observation programs; and space transportation.

Each major section in this volume and the two to follow is introduced by an overview essay, prepared either by a member of the project team or by an individual particularly well-qualified to write on the topic. In the main, these essays are intended to introduce and complement the documents in the section and to place them in a chronological and substantive context. In certain instances the essays go beyond this basic goal to reinterpret specific aspects of the history of the civil space program and to offer historiographical commentary or inquiry about the space program. Each essay contains references to the documents in the section it introduces, and many also contain references to documents in other sections of the collection. These introductory essays were the responsibility of their individual authors, and the views and conclusions contained therein do not necessarily represent the opinions of either George Washington University or NASA.

The documents appended to each chapter were chosen by the essay writer in concert with the editorial team from the more than 2,000 assembled by the research staff for the overall project. The contents of this volume emphasize primary documents or long-out-of-print essays or articles and material from the private recollections of important actors in shaping space affairs. The contents of this volume thus do not comprise in themselves a comprehensive historical account; they must be supplemented by other sources, those both already available and to become available in the future. Indeed, a few of the documents included in this collection are not complete; some portions of them are still subject to security classification. As this collection was being prepared, the U.S. government was involved in declassifying and releasing to the public a number of formerly highly classified documents from the period before 1963. As this declassification process continues, increasingly more information on the early history of NASA and the civil space program will come to light.

The documents included in each section are for the most part arranged chronologically, and each document is assigned its own number in terms of the section in which it is placed. As a result, the first document in the third section of the collection is designated "Document III-1." Each document is accompanied by a headnote setting out its context and providing a background narrative. These headnotes also provide specific information about people and events discussed, as well as bibliographical information about the documents themselves. We have avoided the inclusion of explanatory notes in the documents themselves and have confined such material to the headnotes. The editorial method we adopted for dealing with these documents seeks to preserve spelling, grammar, paragraphing, and use of language as in the original. We have sometimes changed punctuation where it enhances readability. We have used ellipses to note sections of a document not included in this publication, and we have avoided including words and phrases that had been deleted in the original document unless they contribute to an understanding of what was going on in the mind of the writer in making the record. Marginal notations on the original documents are inserted into the text of the documents in brackets, each clearly marked as a marginal comment. When deletions to the original document have been made in the process of declassification, we have noted this with a parenthetical statement in brackets. Except insofar as illustrations and figures are necessary to understanding the text, those items have been omitted from this printed version. Copies of all documents in their original form, however, are available for research by any interested person at the NASA History Office or the Space Policy Institute of George Washington University.

We recognize that there are certain to be quite significant documents left out of this compilation. No two individuals would totally agree on all documents to be included from the more than 2,000 that we collected, and surely we have not been totally successful in locating all relevant records. As a result, this documentary history can raise an immediate question from its users: why were some documents included while others of seemingly equal importance were omitted? There can never be a fully satisfactory answer to this question. Our own criteria for choosing particular documents and omitting others rested on three interrelated factors:

❖ Is the document the best available, most expressive, most representative reflection of a particular event or development important to the evolution of the space program?

❖ Is the document not easily accessible except in one or a few locations, or is it included (for example, in published compilations of presidential statements) in reference sources that are widely available and thus not a candidate for inclusion in this collection?

❖ Is the document protected by copyright, security classification, or some other form of proprietary right and thus unavailable for publication?

Ultimately, as project director I was responsible for the decisions about which documents to include and for the accuracy of the headnotes accompanying them. It has been an occasionally frustrating but consistently exciting experience to be involved with this undertaking; I and my associates hope that those who consult it in the future find our efforts worthwhile.

John M. Logsdon
Director
Space Policy Institute
Elliott School of International Affairs
George Washington University

Biographies of Volume I Essay Authors

R. Cargill Hall is Chief of the Contract Histories Program at the Center for Air Force History in Washington, D.C. He received a B.A. in political science from Whitman College in Walla Walla, Washington, and an M.A. in political science/international relations from San Jose State University. Hall served as a historian for Lockheed Missiles and Space Company (1959-1967) before moving to the California Institute of Technology's Jet Propulsion Laboratory as historian (1967-1977). He joined the U.S. Air Force history program at the headquarters of the Strategic Air Command (1977-1980), subsequently serving as deputy command historian at the headquarters of the Military Airlift Command (1980-1981) and as chief of the Research Division and deputy director of the U.S. Air Force Historical Research Agency (1981-1989), before assuming his present duties. Since the mid-1980s he has assisted other federal history programs focused on aeronautics and astronautics, including those of the National Air and Space Museum and NASA. Hall is the author of *Lunar Impact: A History of Project Ranger* (NASA SP-4210, 1977), editor and contributor to *Lightning Over Bougainville* (Smithsonian Institution Press, 1991), and series editor of the history symposia of the International Academy of Astronautics. He has contributed chapters to and published numerous articles on space law and the history of aeronautics and astronautics in diverse books and journals. He is also contributing editor of *Space Times,* the magazine of the American Astronautical Society, and of *Air & Space Smithsonian.* Hall is a member of the International Academy of Astronautics, the International Institute of Space Law, and he serves on the board of advisors for the Smithsonian Institution Press History of Aviation book series.

Sylvia Katherine Kraemer is a senior executive of NASA's Office of Policy and Plans. Dr. Kraemer joined NASA in 1983 as Director of NASA's History Office. She received her doctorate in the history of ideas from The John Hopkins University in 1969. From 1969 to 1983, she served successively on the faculties of Vassar College, Southern Methodist University, and the University of Maine at Orono. Her many invited lectures and publications include: "Expertise Against Politics: Technology as Ideology on Capitol Hill, 1966-1972" in *Science, Technology, and Human Values* (1983); "The Ideology of Science During the Nixon Years: 1970-76" in *Social Studies of Science* (1984); and "2001 to 1994: Political Environment and the Design of NASA's Space Station System" in *Technology and Culture* (1988), winner of the James Madison Prize of the Society for History in the Federal Government. Her book-length group profile of NASA's Apollo era engineers, *NASA Engineers and the Age of Apollo* (NASA SP-4104), was published in 1992. She co-edited, with Martin J. Collins, *A Spacefaring Nation: Perspectives on American Space History and Policy* (Smithsonian Institution Press, 1991) and *Space: Discovery and Exploration* (Hugh Lauter Levin Associates, Inc., for the Smithsonian Institution, 1993).

Roger D. Launius has been NASA's chief historian at Washington headquarters since 1990. Before that Dr. Launius worked for eight years as a civilian historian with the U.S. Air Force. A graduate of Graceland College, Lamoni, Iowa, he received his Ph.D. from Louisiana State University, Baton Rouge, in 1982. He is the author of articles on the history of aeronautics and space appearing in several journals. He has also published *Joseph Smith III: Pragmatic Prophet* (University of Illinois Press, 1988); *MAC and the Legacy of the Berlin Airlift* (U.S. Air Force, 1989); *Anything, Anywhere, Anytime: An Illustrated History of the Military Airlift Command, 1941-1991* (U.S. Air Force, 1991); *Differing Visions: Dissenters in Mormon History* (University of Illinois Press, 1994); and *NASA: A History of the U.S. Civil Space Program* (Krieger Publishing Co., 1994). He has written or edited six other books. He is currently conducting research for a book-length study of the development of aviation in the American West, covering the period from 1903 to 1945.

John M. Logsdon is Director of both the Center for International Science and Technology Policy and the Space Policy Institute of George Washington University's Elliott School of International Affairs, where he is also Professor of Political Science and International Affairs. He holds a B.S. in physics from Xavier University and a Ph.D. in political science from New York University. He has been at George Washington University since 1970, and he previously taught at The Catholic University of America. Dr. Logsdon's research interests include space policy, the history of the U.S. space program, the structure and process of government decision-making for research and development programs, and international science and technology policy. He is author of *The Decision to Go to the Moon: Project Apollo and the National Interest* (MIT Press, 1970) and has written numerous articles and reports on space policy and science and technology policy. In January 1992 Dr. Logsdon was appointed to Vice President Dan Quayle's Space Policy Advisory Board and served through January 1993. He is a member of the International Academy of Astronautics, of the Board of Advisors of The Planetary Society, of the Board of Directors of the National Space Society, and of the Aeronautics and Space Engineering Board of the National Research Council. In past years he was a member of the National Academy of Sciences's National Academy of Engineering Committee on Space Policy and the National Research Council Committee on a Commercially Developed Space Facility, NASA's Space and Earth Science Advisory Committee and History Advisory Committee, and the Research Advisory Committee of the National Air and Space Museum. He also is a former chair of the Committee on Science and Public Policy of the American Association for the Advancement of Science and of the Education Committee of the International Astronautical Federation. He is a fellow of the American Association for the Advancement of Science and the Explorers Club, as well as an associate fellow of the American Institute of Aeronautics and Astronautics. In addition, he is North American editor for the journal *Space Policy*.

Glossary

ABMA .... Army Ballistic Missile Agency
ACDA .... Arms Control and Disarmament Agency
ACJP .... Air Corps Jet Propulsion
AEC .... Atomic Energy Commission
AF .... Air Force
Ag .... Agriculture
AID .... Agency for International Development
AIS .... American Interplanetary Society
AMPS .... Atmospheric Magnetospheric and Plasmas in Space
AMR .... Atlantic Missile Range
AP .... Associated Press
APT .... Automatic Picture Transmission
ARC .... Ames Research Center
ARPA .... Advanced Research Projects Agency
ARS .... American Rocket Society
AS .... Ascent Stage (LEM)
ASAT .... Antisatellite
ASEB .... Aeronautics and Space Engineering Board
ASP .... LEM Ascent Stage and LEM Descent Stage Propulsion
ASTP .... Advance Space Technology Program
AT&T .... American Telephone & Telegraph
ATS .... Applications Technology Satellite
Autour de la Lune .... *Around the Moon*
BIS .... British Interplanetary Society
BMC .... Ballistic Missile Command
BOB .... Bureau of the Budget
CAB .... Change Analysis Board
CASPER .... Committee on Space Research
CCCB .... Configuration Change Control Board
CCD .... Charge Coupled Device
CIA .... Central Intelligence Agency
CIT .... California Institute of Technology
CoF .... Construction of Facilities
Convair .... Consolidated Vaunt Aircraft
CORI .... Coaxial Reference Interferometer
CSAGI .... Special Committee for the International Geophysical Year
CTS .... Canadian Technology Satellite
DCAS .... Defense Contract Management Command
DCI .... Director of Central Intelligence
De la Terre à la Lune .... *From the Earth to the Moon*
De Mirabilibus Mundi ...... *On the Wonders of the World*
DEW .... Distant Early Warning
DFRC .... Dryden Flight Research Center
Die Rakete zu den
Planetenraumen .... *The Rocket in Planetary Space*
DOC .... Department of Commerce
DOD .... Department of Defense
DOT .... Department of Transportation
E pur si muove .... Yet it does move
EC .... European Community
EEO .... Equal Opportunity Office
ELINT .... Electronic Intelligence
ELV .... Expendable Launch Vehicle
EOR .... Earth Orbital Rendezvous

MRB	Material Review Board
MSFC	Marshall Space Flight Center
MTPE	Mission to Planet Earth
NACA	National Advisory Committee for Aeronautics
NAPA	National Academy of Public Administration
NAS	National Academy of Sciences
NASA	National Aeronautics and Space Administration
NASC	National Aeronautics and Space Council
NATO	North Atlantic Treaty Organization
Nauchnoye Obozreniye	*Science Review*
NDRC	National Defense Research Council
NEES	Naval Engineering Experiment Station
NERVA	Nuclear Engine for Rocket Vehicle Application
NIH	National Institutes of Health
NMSG	NASA Management Study Group
NOA	New Obligational Authority
NOAA	National Oceanic and Atmospheric Administration
NOL	Naval Ordnance Laboratory
NOSS	National Oceanic Satellite System
NRC	National Research Council
NRL	National Research Laboratory
NRO	National Reconnaissance Office
NSC	National Security Council
NSDD	National Security Decision Directive
NSF	National Science Foundation
NST	Nuclear and Space Talks
NSTL	National Space Technology Laboratory
NTIA	National Telecommunications and Information Administration
OAO	Orbiting Astronomical Observatories
OAST	Office of Aeronautics and Space Technology
ODM	Office of Defense Mapping
OEO	Office of Economic Opportunity
OFT	Orbiter Flight Test
OGO	Orbiting Geophysical Observatories
OMSF	Office of Manned Space Flight
ONR	Office of Naval Research
OSO	Orbiting Solar Observatory
OSSA	Office of Space Science and Applications
OST	Office of Space Technology
OSTP	Office of Science Technology Policy
OTA	Optical Telescope Assembly
OTP	Office of Technology Policy
P-E	Perkin-Elmer
PAD	Program Approval Document
PMR	Pacific Missile Range
PSAC	President's Science Advisory Committee
R&LO	Reliability and Launch Operations
R&D	Research and Development
R&PM	Research and Program Management
R&T	Research and Technology
RATO	Rocket Assisted Take Off
RCA	Radio Corporation of America
RDT&E	Research, Development, Test, and Evaluation
RIF	Reduction in Force
RMI	Reaction Motors, Inc.
RNC	Reflective Null Corrector

Sat .... Saturn
Sidereus Nuncius .... Sidereal Messenger
SIG .... Senior Interagency Group
Somnium .... *Dream*
SPB .... Standard Practice Bulletin
SRM .... Solid Rocket Motor
STG .... Space Task Group
STS .... Space Transportation System
T&DA .... Training and Data Acquisition
TAN .... Task Authorization Notice
TAOS .... Thrust Assisted Orbiter Shuttle
TCP .... Technological Capabilities Panel
TMIS .... Technical Management Information System
TP .... Transition Period
TV .... Television
USA .... United States of America
UCLA .... University of California at Los Angeles
UFO .... Unidentified Flying Object
ULV .... Unmanned Launch Vehicles
UN .... United Nations
UNESCO .... United Nations Educational Scientific, and Cultural Organization
URSI .... International Scientific Radio Union
U.S. .... United States
USAF .... U.S. Air Force
USC .... University of Southern California
USGS .... United States Geological Survey
USNC .... United States National Committee
USSR .... Union of Soviet Socialist Republics
UV .... Ultra Violet
Verein fur
Raumschiffahrt .... Society for Spaceship Travel, or VfR
Voyage dans la Lune .... *The Voyage to the Moon*
WAC .... Womens Auxiliary Corps, Without Attitude Control
WFC .... Wallops Flight Center
WFF .... Wallops Flight Facility
XCMS .... Experimental Command and Service Module

CPSIA information can be obtained
at www.ICGtesting.com
Printed in the USA
LVHW111610310122
709865LV00011B/915